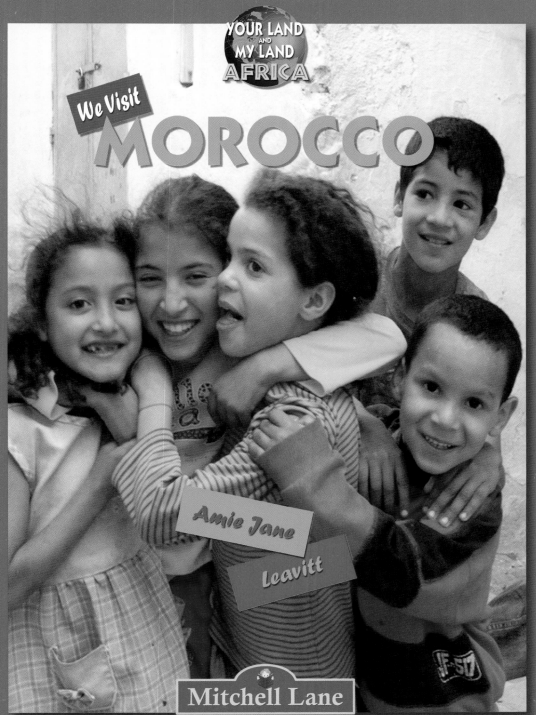

YOUR LAND AND MY LAND
AFRICA

We Visit
MOROCCO

Amie Jane
Leavitt

Mitchell Lane
PUBLISHERS
P.O. Box 196
Hockessin, Delaware 19707

YOUR LAND
AND
MY LAND
AFRICA

Egypt
Ethiopia
Ghana
Kenya
Libya
Madagascar
Morocco
Nigeria
Rwanda
South Africa

YOUR LAND AND MY LAND
AFRICA

We Visit
MOROCCO

LIBYA

EGYPT

Aswān

SUDAN

Gulf of Aden

Addis
Ababa

Printing   1   2   3   4   5   6   7   8   9

Library of Congress Cataloging-in-Publication Data
Leavitt, Amie Jane.
  We visit Morocco / by Amie Jane Leavitt.
      p. cm. -- (Your land and my land. Africa)
  Includes bibliographical references and index.
  ISBN 978-1-61228-306-7 (library bound)
1. Morocco—Juvenile literature. I. Title. II. Series: Your land and my land
(Mitchell Lane Publishers). Africa.
  DT305.L39 2012
  964—dc23
                                                          2012009625
eBook ISBN: 9781612283807

PUBLISHER'S NOTE: This story is based on the author's extensive research,
which she believes to be accurate. Documentation of this research is on
page 61.

    The internet sites referenced herein were active as of the publication date.
Due to the fleeting nature of some websites, we cannot guarantee they will all
be active when you are reading this book.

Contents

Introduction.. 6
1 The Hollywood of North Africa 9
    Where in the World Is Morocco? 11
    Facts at a Glance 13
2 A Rich History and Government 15
3 Moroccans Today 21
4 At Home in Morocco 25
5 From Sea to Shining Sea 33
6 Mountain Peaks and Berber Villages.. 39
7 The Great Cities of the Plains 43
8 Roughing it in the Sahara 49
9 Dreaming of Morocco 55
Moroccan Recipe: Moroccan Couscous 56
Moroccan Craft: Hamsa Bookmark 57
Timeline 58
Chapter Notes.. 60
Further Reading 61
    Books 61
    On the Internet 61
    Works Consulted 61
Glossary.. 62
Index 63

Introduction

Africa is an intriguing continent. There are tropical jungles near the equator. Savannas and grasslands dot the south. Island nations are found in both the east and the west. The remnants of ancient civilizations are preserved along the Nile. And the Sahara, one of the world's largest deserts, spreads across the north. Africa is known for its natural resources, its geographic wonders, and its amazing wildlife. The continent teems with such fascinating creatures as lions, giraffes, zebras, elephants, chimpanzees, monkeys, hippopotamuses, gorillas, leopards, camels, and rhinoceros.

Marrakesh, Morocco

Morocco

AFRICA

Africa is one of the earth's seven continents. It has more countries than any other continent on earth, with a total of fifty-seven. Some of the countries that you're probably most familiar with are Egypt, South Africa, Nigeria, Congo, Ethiopia, Kenya, and, of course, Morocco.

Morocco is a country that is located in the far western corner of North Africa. It is part of the Western Hemisphere. Since it is only 9 miles (14 kilometers) away from Spain by water, Morocco is also the closest African country to Europe. And because of its location, Morocco has always been influenced by African, European, and Arab cultures.

Tangier is located on Morocco's Mediterranean coast, just a quick ferry ride away from Spain. Many travelers arriving from Europe begin their Moroccan journey here.

The Hollywood of North Africa

Welcome to Morocco! Or as the Moroccans say in Arabic, *Marhaba Fi El-Maghreb!* You might be surprised to know that Morocco is actually considered the Hollywood of North Africa. It's true. Dozens of movies have been filmed on location here in Morocco. *The Mummy* and *The Mummy Returns* were both filmed here. So were parts of the movies *Prince of Persia: The Sands of Time, What a Girl Wants, The Bourne Ultimatum, Gladiator, Mamma Mia, Alexander, Black Hawk Down, Lawrence of Arabia, Sahara,* Alfred Hitchcock's *The Man Who Knew Too Much,* and many others. Some people think that Morocco was also the location of the first *Star Wars.* Unfortunately, it was not. Morocco may look like Luke Skywalker's home planet of Tatooine, but this fictional place was actually set in another North African country, Tunisia.

Why are so many movies filmed here? Movie producers choose Morocco for many reasons. For one, it's inexpensive to film here. For another, the government is quite easy to work with. And still another, movie sets built on Morocco's landscape can be made to look like places from all over the world. Movies set in Nepal, Tibet, Egypt, Jerusalem, Jordan, Bethlehem, and even New Mexico have been filmed here. So, the next time you see a movie that is set in a desert or mountainous landscape, ask yourself: could this be Morocco?

A Moroccan in Hollywood

Sanaa Hamri was born in northern Morocco in the town of Tangier. At age seventeen, she left Morocco on a college scholarship to Sarah Lawrence College in New York to study acting and theater. She tried to get her break as an actress after college graduation, but she didn't get far. By the year 2000, she realized she might need to do things differently if she wanted to stay in the business. She decided that it might still be possible to make a living in the film industry that she loved, but in a different way. She started looking at other possibilities, including video editing. She spent hours teaching herself the complicated Avid video editing machine. "I just opened the manual up and started on page one! I had never taken a filmmaking course—and I still haven't taken one," she admitted.[1] But she was good at it, very good. She decided to make editing and directing her career.

Hamri has directed music videos for such artists as Mariah Carey, Prince, Sting, Christina Aguilera, Alicia Keys, and Jay-Z. She has also directed episodes of popular television shows (*Men in Trees, Desperate Housewives,* and *Grey's Anatomy*) and full-length motion pictures (*Something New, Just Wright,* and *The Sisterhood of the Traveling Pants 2*). She would eventually like to direct movies to show the world what daily life in Morocco is really like.

Hamri credits her success partly to her positive attitude. "I really believe that the first philosophy of life [is] you create your reality," she said. "If you believe it's going to be difficult for you to do anything, it will be… If I had that attitude, I would not be where I am."[2]

The Cold Country with a Hot Sun

Morocco is known as the cold country with a hot sun. In some parts of the country there are very tall mountains that are snowcapped in the winter and spring. In other parts of the country, the weather—especially in the summer—is extremely hot. You've heard of the Sahara

FYI FACT:

In the 7th century C.E., the Prophet Muhammad founded the great Islamic Empire. This empire eventually stretched from Afghanistan in the east to Morocco in the west. Morocco was the last country in the empire to see the sun set each evening. So, it became known as the "land of the setting sun."

WHERE IN THE WORLD IS MOROCCO?

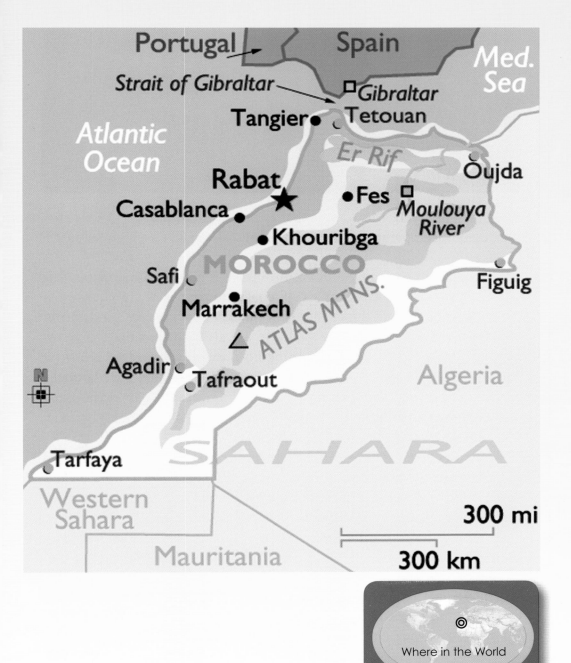

Portugal

Spain

Med. Sea

Strait of Gibraltar

Gibraltar

Tangier

Tetouan

Atlantic Ocean

Er Rif

Oujda

Rabat

Casablanca

Fes

Moulouya River

Khouribga

Safi

MOROCCO

Figuig

Marrakech

ATLAS MTNS.

Agadir

Tafraout

Algeria

Tarfaya

SAHARA

Western Sahara

300 mi

300 km

Mauritania

Where in the World

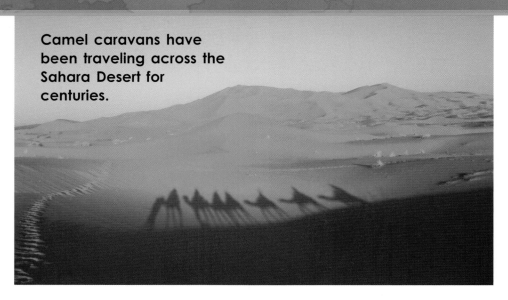

Camel caravans have been traveling across the Sahara Desert for centuries.

Desert, right? Well, Morocco is the farthest western part of this swelter-ing region. Temperatures here can sometimes reach as high as 120°F (49°C).

Morocco's geography and culture make it a captivating place. The country has hundreds of miles of coastline. It has vast expanses of desert with huge sand dunes that shift quickly during fierce sandstorms. It also has mountains. Some of these are so high that they're snow-capped for much of the year. Imagine returning home to tell your friends you went skiing or snowboarding in Africa one day, bounced across the rust-red sand dunes of the Sahara atop a camel the next, and then went surfing in the Atlantic's turquoise blue waters the next. Yes, this is all possible in Morocco.

When people visit parts of Morocco, they feel as if they've stepped back in time. Picture in your mind a colorful bazaar with shiny bronze genie lamps, fringe-edged magic carpets, flute-playing snake charmers, acrobats, magicians, veiled women casting fortunes, and donkeys toting supplies. This is not only the Morocco of the past, it is the Morocco of the present, too.

All of this and more awaits you in this enchanting and mysterious North African country. Whether you get to visit Morocco in person, or just in the pages of this book, you will not be disappointed by the many adventures that await you.

MOROCCO FACTS AT A GLANCE

Moroccan Flag

Full name: Kingdom of Morocco

Languages: Arabic (official), Berber languages, French (often the language of business, government, and diplomacy)

Population: 32,309,239 (July 2012 est.)

Land area: 172,317 square miles (446,300 square kilometers); slightly larger than California

Capital: Rabat

Government: constitutional monarchy

Ethnic makeup: Arab-Berber 99%, other 1%

Religions: Muslim 99%, Christian 1%, Jewish 0.02%

Exports: clothing and textiles, electric components, inorganic chemicals, transistors, crude minerals, fertilizers (including phosphates), petroleum products, citrus fruits, vegetables, fish

Imports: crude petroleum, textile fabric, telecommunications equipment, wheat, gas and electricity, transistors, plastics

Agricultural Products: barley, wheat, citrus fruits, grapes, vegetables, olives, livestock, wine

Average high temperatures:
   On the coast (Casablanca): January 63°F (17°C); August 79°F (26°C)
   Near the desert (Ouarzazate): January 62°F (17°C); August 99°F (37°C)
   In the mountains (Ifrane): January 48°F (9°C); August 86°F (30°C)

Average annual rainfall:
   On the coast (Casablanca): 16.7 inches (42.5 centimeters)
   Near the desert (Ouarzazate): 4.5 inches (11.4 centimeters)
   In the mountains (Ifrane): 44 inches (111.8 centimeters)

Highest point: Jebel Toubkal—13,665 feet (4,165 meters)

Longest river: Draa River—700 miles (1,100 kilometers)

Flag: Designed in 1912, the flag is solid red with a green five-pointed star called a pentacle in the center. This star is known as Sulayman's (Solomon's) seal. An Arab country, Morocco uses red and green—traditional Arab colors—in its flag. The star represents the five pillars of Islam, connecting Morocco to the Muslim world. The star also signifies the association of God and nation.

National sport: Morocco doesn't have an official national sport. But Moroccans do love football (soccer) and have a national football team called the Atlas Lions.

National animal: Barbary lion

Source: *CIA World Factbook:* Morocco

Nomadic peoples make their shelters wherever they can. Here, a shelter was built around a tree using materials provided by the land.

A Rich History and Government

Step back in time thousands of years to the exotic lands of the Middle East. A group of nomads has just finished loading their camels with blankets, food, water, and supplies. Now, they're ready to begin their journey across the rolling sand dunes of the great desert. Days and weeks pass. They suffer under the sweltering heat. To protect themselves from the scorching sun, they cover their faces and heads with veils and turbans. They endure the fierce winds of swirling sandstorms. They trudge over cinnamon-colored dunes leading their noble dromedaries behind them.

In the distance, they often spy what they think is an oasis. Sometimes they are right and they arrive at an island of swaying palms and lush pools of water surrounded on all sides by sand. They stop and relax under the trees and drink water from the refreshing crystal-clear springs. Other times, they are wrong. The sun has played a trick on their eyes and what they thought was an oasis was just a mirage. There is no water and no green palms, just a sea of what seems to be never-ending sand.

After many weeks of traveling, the nomads finally come to a great ocean. They have crossed the entire Sahara Desert and have ended up in what is known today as the Kingdom of Morocco. Some of these nomads will stay and make a life here. Others will continue traveling back and forth across the Sahara in camel caravans peddling goods and supplies to people along the way.

The Berber women of the Rif Mountains wear traditional clothing from hand-woven textiles and straw hats to protect themselves from the intense Moroccan sun.

Free People

There are many stories like this one that attempt to explain how the original inhabitants of Morocco arrived here. Yet, that's just what they are, stories. No one knows for sure where the original inhabitants of Morocco came from or how they got here. One thing is for certain, though; the original settlers did have a name. They called themselves *Imazighen*. This is translated to mean "the free people." And free they were. Free from formal governmental rule. Free to move about the land as they pleased. The Berber people of North Africa today—many of whom live in Morocco—are the descendants of these ancient people. The Berber people may have not always been able to maintain their freedom from governmental rule. But they have been able to hold on to their traditional culture as they have adopted things here and there from their ruling nations.

The region now known as Morocco has been ruled by many groups of people throughout its history. That's mostly because of its strategic location at the point where the Mediterranean Sea and Atlantic Ocean meet, a crossroads of trade.

Sometime around 800 B.C.E., historians believe that a group of people called the Phoenicians arrived in Morocco and began establishing colonies that they mainly used as trading posts. The ruins of one of these ancient colonies can still be visited today. Called Lixus, the former settlement is now known as Larache, and is located on the Atlantic coast, just south of Tangier. There's not much of it left. It's mainly just a rubble of rocks, toppling chimney stacks, and the crumbling foundations of the ancient buildings.

From the first century C.E. until the 600s, a variety of peoples inhabited Morocco. First came the Romans, then peoples from the Iberian Peninsula (Spain) known as the Visigoths. Then, the Vandals came from the area that is now known as Germany. Many of these groups of peoples took over the original Phoenician colonies and cities. Lixus, for example, was not only inhabited by the Phoenicians, but also by the Romans. And the Greeks based their famous mythological Garden of the Hesperides here in Lixus. It was in this garden that the keepers of the golden apples were believed to be found.

Toward the end of the 7th century, Morocco was invaded by the Arabs under the leadership of Uqba ibn Nafi. This Arab general was actually responsible for the Arab invasion of most of North Africa. The Arab invasion brought with it something that would prove life-changing for the Berbers in Morocco: the Islamic religion. But while most Berbers converted to Islam, they kept their traditional laws and customs. In 743, the Berbers of Morocco drove out their Arab rulers and remained free from foreign rule for nearly a thousand years. But the Islamic influence in Morocco continues to this day.

In the 1800s, Spain and France both showed an interest in controlling Morocco. They, too, recognized the region as a very important place politically, economically, and militarily. From the late 1800s until the mid-1900s, part of Morocco was controlled by Spain and the other part was controlled by France. After World War II, the Moroccans were finally able to gain their independence on March 2, 1956.

Once Morocco had become an independent nation, the leaders decided to establish a constitutional monarchy. This is a type of government where the country has both a constitution and a parliament. But instead of an elected president, it is ruled by a king or queen. The United Kingdom, Japan, Sweden, and Thailand are examples of other constitutional monarchies. In 1961, a man named Hassan II became king of Morocco. Because of his lineage in the Alaouite Dynasty, he is believed to be a direct descendant of the Prophet Muhammad, the founder of Islam.

Hassan II

King Hassan II ruled Morocco from March 3, 1961, until his death on July 23, 1999. Prior to becoming king, Hassan II was educated at the Imperial College at Rabat where he studied language. He later received a law degree from the University of Bordeaux in France.

King Hassan II wrote Morocco's first constitution in 1962. This was a positive step forward for the country that produced a more democratic government. The constitution provided for more freedom of the press and religion and also allowed for a legislature to be elected by the people. However, the king didn't give up all of his power with this new constitution. He could still hire and fire the Prime Minister, he could dissolve the legislature if he wanted to, and he had absolute control over the army. This ended up causing problems for the king throughout his reign.

King Hassan II

FYI FACT:

In Greek mythology, the Hesperides were goddesses of the evening. They were daughters of the Titan Atlas. They lived in a beautiful garden that was located on the western edge of the Olympian world, in the area now known as Morocco. This was the garden of the gods. It grew many magical plants including one apple tree that produced golden apples. The golden glow of these apples created some of the most beautiful sunsets in the Greek world. When eaten, the golden flesh of these apples was believed to make the gods immortal.

Many people wanted to come and eat the fruit of the golden apple tree, but this was strictly forbidden. The gift of immortality could not just be given to anyone. So, the Hesperides had one main responsibility. They were to care for the garden and protect it from invaders. They had a hundred-headed dragon named Ladon to help them in this charge.

One of King Hassan II's goals was to help improve the relations between Arabs and Israelis. He truly wanted these two groups of people to find a way to live peacefully with each other. While he wanted to see peace between these groups around the world, he was also concerned with peace within his own country since there were both Arabs and Jews that considered themselves Moroccans. During his reign, King Hassan II often helped set up meetings between Arab and Israeli world leaders in an effort to establish peace agreements in the Middle East.

Following King Hassan II's death in 1999, his son Mohammed VI became King. On June 17, 2011, Mohammed VI introduced a new constitution for the country. This new constitution gave more power to the legislature. It also set up a judiciary system that is free from control by either the king or the legislature. The constitution took away the king's right to dissolve the legislature. It also protected basic rights of people including freedom of thought, ideas, artistic expression, and creation. In addition, women were guaranteed both civic and social equality with men. Political experts around the world hope that this new constitution is a step in a very positive direction not only for Morocco but for the rest of the Arab world.[1]

Casablanca is a thriving port city in Morocco. The Boulevard de Paris, shown here, is a major thoroughfare in the city. French place names are common in Morocco, reminders of the country's history as a French colony.

Chapter

3

Moroccans Today

More than 32 million people live in Morocco today. Ninety-nine percent of these people claim to have Arab and Berber ancestry. Ninety-nine percent of the population are also practicing Muslims.

Morocco's official language is Arabic. But many Moroccans speak at least three languages: Arabic, a Berber language, and French. Since Morocco is so close to Spain, some Moroccans in the north also speak Spanish. And because of the growth of tourism, many Moroccans are learning English, too. It's definitely possible to find Moroccans who can speak five languages fluently. Just imagine how many people you could communicate with if you could speak that many languages yourself!

A little over half of the population of Morocco lives in cities. The rest live in small villages in the countryside. The people who live in cities work many different kinds of jobs. In more modern cities, like Casablanca, people work in jobs very similar to the jobs you'd find in any European or American city. In some of the more traditional cities, though, many people work in service jobs in hotels and restaurants. They also work as tour guides and entertainers. Many urban dwellers also have their own businesses. They sell merchandise or food from pushcarts. They make handicrafts, jewelry, and clothing to sell, too.

Many of the jobs in Morocco are in agriculture. Along the Atlantic and Mediterranean coastlines, more than 100,000 people work in the fishing industry. In fact, Morocco has the largest fish market in all of Africa. In the plains, farming is king. Moroccan farmers grow barley, wheat, citrus fruits, grapes, vegetables, and olives. Herdsmen raise

Most of the sheep in Morocco are native to the region. Sheep are raised here mainly for meat; wool is merely a by-product.

livestock like sheep and goats. Many of Morocco's agricultural goods are sold to other places, especially to Europe.

Many Moroccans are also employed in industrial, mining, and manufacturing jobs. Mining is a very important industry in Morocco, especially the mining of phosphates. Morocco is the third-largest producer of phosphates in the world. Phosphate minerals are used in fertilizers, which are very important in agriculture. The territory of Western Sahara is very rich in phosphates. That's part of the reason why Morocco and its neighbors to the south have been arguing over their borders for years.

Moroccans dress in a conservative style. This is mainly because of their Islamic faith. Most women wear scarves over their heads. Yet, they don't often cover their entire faces as women do in more strict Muslim nations. Men will often wear some kind of hat too. Sometimes they'll wear a colorful knit hat. Other times they will wear a red flat-topped cone hat called a *fez*. Both men and women wear outer robes called *djellabas*. They will also wear the traditional Moroccan footwear called *babouches*. These colorful shoes are made out of soft Moroccan leather and slip on and off like slippers.

Princess Lalla Salma

In 2002, Salma Bennani married King Mohammed VI. With this marriage, she became the very first commoner in Moroccan history to marry a king. She also became the first princess in Morocco to ever be officially named. Up until this point, it was Moroccan tradition that the king did not reveal the name of his bride in public. Mohammed VI was the first to change this by officially announcing his marriage to Salma Bennani and allowing pictures of them in their wedding attire to be published by the media.

Salma Bennani was born in Fes. Her father was a school teacher. Her mother died when she was only three years old, so she was raised by her grandmother. She went to private school in Rabat and then went on to earn a Baccalaureate in mathematics and science at the Lycée Hassan II (a university named for her future father-in-law). She continued her education, receiving a graduate degree in computer science. She was working as a computer engineer at Omnium North Africa when she met King Mohammed VI at a private party.

Salma Bennani instantly became a trendsetter in Morocco. Many Moroccan women are inspired by her rise from the common life to that of royalty.

FYI FACT:

When the Romans controlled Morocco, they set up their capital in a town called Volubilis. The ruins of this ancient Roman city are found near the city of Fes. Visitors can see crumbling Roman columns, stone archways, roads, mosaics, and the remains of the old capitol building.

The Al-Karaouine Mosque is located in Fes, Morocco. Approximately 22,000 people can worship together at the same time in this massive structure. The mosque's school became an official state university in 1963.

At Home in Morocco

You might be wondering what everyday life is like in Morocco for the people who live there. You'd be surprised to find out that in many ways, they are just like you. They spend time with family and friends, they go to school and work, and they move about their communities using many different types of transportation. They even celebrate holidays and watch sporting events just like people all over the world.

Time for School

Both boys and girls go to school in Morocco. Children begin school at age six. They must complete at least nine years of school. After that, they can choose to continue, and many do. More than 200,000 Moroccans attend colleges or universities every year.

There are fourteen public universities in Morocco. The most well-known is Mohammed V University, founded in 1957. Students here study medicine, law, liberal arts, and science. The oldest university in Morocco—and in the whole world for that matter—is the University of Al-Karaouine. It was established in 859 C.E., and students come here from all over the world to study Islam. Al Akhawayn University is another important university in Morocco. Founded in 1995, it is the first private English university in North Africa. It teaches subjects very similar to the subjects you'd find in a university in the United States.

Planes, Trains, and Automobiles

How do people get around in Morocco? Well, just like many other places on earth, Morocco has planes, trains, and automobiles. The country also has other means of transport such as boats, buses, camels, donkeys, bicycles, and mopeds. The type of transportation a person uses depends on how far they are going and where they are traveling. Many people arrive in Morocco by ferry across the Straits of Gibraltar. Or, they arrive by airplane at one of Morocco's airports. Once in Morocco, people mainly travel between the cities by train and bus. They may also rent cars and drive themselves from place to place. Within the big cities, people will often get around by using the bus system or on their own moped or bicycle. In the old walled portions of the cities (called *medinas*), though, motorized vehicles are not allowed. The lanes are too narrow, so only foot traffic or donkey traffic (to haul goods) is permitted. In the desert, camels are the preferred

Moroccans travel across their country via planes, trains, and automobiles.

method of transportation. When you visit the Sahara, the easiest way to get around is either on foot or on the humped back of one of these majestic "ships of the desert."

What's For Dinner?

Morocco is known around the world for its delicious food. Some of the country's most famous dishes are couscous, tagine, pastilla, and mint tea. Couscous is a grain that North Africans have been eating since the 12th century. You may have tried it before, since it has been popular in the United States for many years now. Tagine is a stew that is cooked in a clay pot with the same name. Pastilla is a meat pie or turnover, with pigeon meat stuffed inside a flaky crust. Mint tea is popular in Morocco. People drink it many times throughout the day and it's almost always offered at meals.

Moroccan food is considered spicy, but not hot. Some of the spices Moroccans use are cumin, saffron, cinnamon, nutmeg, paprika, cardamom, fenugreek, hot and sweet pepper, garlic, parsley, and dill. Look in your kitchen's spice cabinet at home. Do you see any of those names on the jars? What do they look, smell, and taste like?

Moroccans use many different types of meat in their cooking. They use mutton (adult sheep), lamb (young sheep), beef, fish, and chicken. They also use unusual meats like pigeon, rabbit, and even camel. Perhaps the most unusual meat they eat is sheep's head. Yes, they eat the whole thing! Maybe you are brave enough to try these unusual dishes sometime. Or maybe not!

Besides meat, Moroccans also use many different types of vegetables and fruits in their cooking: parsnips, pumpkin, leeks, artichokes, zucchini, eggplant, carrots, figs, dates, almonds, melons, tomatoes, potatoes, olives, oranges, lemons (including pickled lemon), and grapefruit.

Moroccans traditionally eat their largest meal at midday. If everyone is home, they will sit down together as a family at a low table. They don't have chairs. Everyone sits on fluffy cushions on the floor instead.

If you eat with a Moroccan family, don't expect to get your own plate. They eat "family style." That means that a large plate of food is placed in the center of the table, and everyone eats from it. And they usually eat with their fingers, with their right hand only. (*See Chapter 9 for the reason*). A typical Moroccan meal starts off with a variety of salads, followed by tagine. Then, a couscous dish is served. The meal ends with a light dessert of fruit and pastries. And you'll always have a glass of mint tea to wash it all down!

Traditional Moroccan food isn't the only kind of food that Moroccans eat. Remember, the country was ruled by other nations for hundreds of years. So, they also eat traditional foods from those countries. In homes and restaurants across Morocco, both French and Spanish cuisines are popular.

Let's Celebrate!

Since most Moroccans are Muslims, the majority of their festivals and holidays revolve around the Islamic faith. The most important holiday of the year in Morocco is Ramadan, which is the ninth month of the Islamic calendar.

The Islamic calendar is a lunar calendar, which means it is based on the cycle of the moon. Most of the Western world uses the Gregorian calendar which is not based on lunar cycles, but instead has standard months of specific lengths. The Islamic calendar follows the moon's cycle, so it is shorter in length than the Gregorian calendar and changes every year. Because of that, Islamic holidays occur at different times every year when compared to the Gregorian calendar.

Moroccan faithful pray on the esplanade of the Hassan II Mosque in Casablanca on the holy night of Laylat al-Qadr during the month of Ramadan.

Sometimes Ramadan is in July. Sometimes it's in January, and sometimes it's in September.

Ramadan is a special holiday that shows a Muslim's faith and devotion. During Ramadan, Muslims fast from dawn to sunset. This can be up to fifteen hours a day. They don't eat any food or drink any water. Imagine how hard this must be when temperatures soar above 100°F (38°C). On regular days of the year, a Muslim will say prayers five times a day. During Ramadan, they will say even more prayers. They also read extra verses from their holy book, the Quran. The purpose of fasting is to stop focusing on the physical needs of the body, so that the people can focus more on spirituality.

At the end of the month of fasting, the people celebrate with a two- or three-day festival called Eid al-Fitr. This is a splendid time to be in Morocco. The people enjoy grand feasts, dress in new clothing, and tell stories about their ancestors. They play traditional music and dance in colorful costumes. Overall, they just enjoy spending time with their family and friends.

The Islamic New Year is another important religious holiday. It is celebrated on the first day of the Islamic calendar. This holiday is not at all similar to the New Year's Day on the Gregorian calendar where grand celebrations, fireworks, and parties are the norm. For the New Year, Moroccan Muslims reflect on the past year, and make resolutions for the upcoming year.

At various times of year, celebrations called Moussems take place throughout Morocco. Some Moussems celebrate the harvest season (like the Honey Festival in Argana in May, or the Cherry Festival in Sefrou in June), and others are religious celebrations. The Candle Festival in Sale is celebrated every year on the day before Mawlid Al-Nabi, the birthday of the Prophet Muhammad. Moroccans spend months preparing elaborate candles for this festival, which are carried down the street in a procession. Groups of dancers and musicians follow the parade with performances.

Fun and Games

Football, or soccer, is a very popular sport in Morocco. The country even has its own national team, the Atlas Lions, which is considered to be one of the best in Africa. In 2012, the team won its first Arab Nations Cup, beating Libya for the top spot. The Atlas Lions' home stadium is in Marrakesh. It seats 45,000 spectators. Moroccan kids,

The Atlas Lions wear uniforms in the red and green colors of their country's flag.

even those who live in rural villages, are often seen playing football in organized and unorganized teams.

Art and music are important in Moroccan culture. From a very young age, Berber kids learn from their parents how to make handi-crafts like jewelry, leatherworks, and rugs. All of these handmade goods can be found in the *souks* (sooks), or marketplaces, of Moroccan towns and cities. Many Moroccan children, especially in rural areas, are taught how to sing and dance to the country's folk music. They might also learn how to play some of the traditional instruments like lutes, rababs, cymbals, flutes, and drums.

Moroccans are known for storytelling. In their culture, storytellers are called *halakis.* These old sages tell ancient tales that have been passed on from one generation to the next over many centuries. They tell of wise men and fools, snake charmers, belly dancers, sultans, genies, and mystics. But this tradition of telling stories might not be around forever. Most of the halakis today are old men. And not many young Moroccans want to become halakis—they want to be part of the modern world instead.[1]

Many people arrive in Morocco from Europe by ferry. Ferries can transport both passengers and cars.

From Sea to Shining Sea

Now that we know a little about Morocco and its people, let's take a tour of some of the country's most fascinating places.

Morocco is usually divided into four geographic regions. The first consists of the Mediterranean and Atlantic Coastlines. The second region is the area that contains the Rif and Atlas Mountains. The third is called the Great Cities of the Plains. And the fourth is the Sahara Desert. We're going to start our tour at the northern coast and then we'll make our way around the country to each of the other three regions.

Arriving by Ferry

One way to get to northern Morocco is to take a ferry from Spain. A ferry is a boat that transports both people and automobiles. The ferry ride from Spain to Morocco takes anywhere from a half an hour to an hour and a half. It just depends on what kind of boat you take and where you leave from. If you want a really long ride on a ferry, you can take one from France. These ferries take about thirty-six hours to reach the shores of Morocco.

Morocco's coastline stretches 1,140 miles (1,835 kilometers). It begins along the Mediterranean sea in the north and continues to the Atlantic Ocean in the west. Morocco's northern-most point borders another important body of water, the Straits of Gibraltar. This is a narrow passageway that connects the Mediterranean and Atlantic. You can easily see Spain from Morocco's shoreline along the Straits of

FYI FACT:

Spain and Morocco have been trying to figure out if it's possible to build a chunnel, or railroad tube, under the Straits of Gibraltar. This would be similar to the one built under the English Channel that connects England with France. This project would be extremely expensive. It would also be very difficult to construct. So, there's no guarantee it will ever happen. But if it did, people would be able to board a train in Spain, go underground (and underwater), and a short time later arrive above ground in Morocco.[1]

Gibraltar. You'll see quite a traffic jam in this area, too—more than 300 ships pass through the straits every day.

When you arrive by ferry, Tangier is likely the first city you'll see. This port town was once considered the "Pearl of the Mediterranean." It was a major stop for boat traffic. Today, Tangier is a bit of a rough town. Yet, there are a few fun things to see and do here. For one, you can check out the kasbah. This is the white fortress that looks out over the city. Back in the 17th century, it was the sultan's palace and the place where people came seeking protection from enemies. Today it is a museum with art and archaeology exhibits. Another place you can visit is the American Legation. This building was given to the United States in 1821 by Sultan Moulay Suliman. It was the first building owned by the United States that was located outside of the country's borders. It's now a cultural center, library, and museum. It's also on the U.S. National Register of Historic Places.

FYI FACT:

The city of Ceuta is located on the Mediterranean coast of Morocco. Yet, it is not controlled by Morocco. It's actually controlled by Spain. On the opposite side of the Mediterranean in Spain, something similar is also true. The city of Gibraltar is not controlled by Spain. It is controlled by the United Kingdom.

Royal Palace of Rabat

Capital City

After leaving Tangier, the next major city to the south is Morocco's capital city of Rabat. Here, visitors can see the royal palace of Morocco's king, who lives in the city. If you come at the right time, you'll get to see the changing of the guards. This is a special ceremony where the soldiers who stand guard at the palace are relieved from their shifts and replaced by new guards.

Rabat may be the capital city. But it is Casablanca, located a little further to the south, that is the largest and most important business center in the country.

Here's Looking At You Kid...

Have you ever heard of the old movie *Casablanca* with Humphrey Bogart and Ingrid Bergman? It's a black-and-white movie about World

FYI FACT:

Morocco's relationship with the United States actually goes back to the very beginning of U.S. history. On December 20, 1777, Morocco became the first country to officially recognize the United States as an independent nation. That was a big deal, since at that time, the Revolutionary War had not even been won yet.

The final scene from *Casablanca*

War II that came out in 1942. Well, as you might guess, the movie was about Morocco's very own Casablanca. However, the movie wasn't filmed here—it was actually filmed in Hollywood. Even so, this movie did make Morocco's coastal city very famous.

Today, Casablanca is one of the most modern cities in all of Morocco. More than three million people live here. Many of the businesses, homes, hotels, and restaurants in Casablanca are similar to the ones you'd find in a European or North American city.

A popular place to visit in Casablanca is the Hassan II Mosque, which opened in 1993. The Hassan II Mosque is the largest mosque in North Africa. It can hold 25,000 people inside the building and 80,000 more on the grounds. Most mosques have a minaret or central tower that has a rounded dome at the top. This tower is used to call Muslims to daily prayer. The minaret on the Hassan II Mosque is the tallest in the world, at 689 feet (210 meters) tall. The Hassan II Mosque is unique in other ways, too. The mosque was built on a platform over the Atlantic. Part of the building has a glass floor which reveals the ocean below. The mosque also has a sliding roof which can be opened to the heavens on special occasions. The Hassan II Mosque is one of only two mosques in Morocco that non-Muslims can visit. But they can only come at certain times of the day. And visitors should always remember to remove their shoes at the door—it's a sign of respect.

Casablanca is a Spanish name. *Casa* means "house" and *blanca* means "white." This is the city of the white houses. Locals just call their city "Casa."

West Coast Surfing

When you think of west coast surfing, you might picture people catching waves in California. But surfing isn't only a popular sport on the West Coast of the United States. It's actually a popular sport on the West Coast of Africa, too. Surfers toting their own boards often fly in from Europe and America to try out the waves on Morocco's Atlantic coast. If you want to learn to surf in Morocco, there are plenty of surf companies in the area that can give you lessons. Some are located in the popular beachfront town of Essaouira (eh-so-WEER-uh).

Essaouira is a beautiful seaside town with white adobe buildings and cobalt blue fishing boats floating in the harbor. People who visit this town like to surf, look for seashells, swim in the ocean, and eat seafood. In Essaouira, just picking out what fish you'll eat is an experience. At the fish auction on the docks, you'll see piles of flat stingrays spread out on trays. You'll watch as sardines, scampi, and snapper spill out of wooden buckets and barrels. The fishermen have lightly sprinkled the fish with sea salt to keep them fresh. After you buy your fish, you take it to a nearby vendor, who will cook it up on his outdoor grill. Then, you eat it at a picnic table right on the beach.

Surfing in Morocco

Jebel Toubkal is the tallest mountain in the Atlas range. It's also the highest peak in North Africa, rising to well over 13,000 feet. Expert hikers claim it's possible to hike to the top in two days.

Mountain Peaks and Berber Villages

Most of northern and central Morocco is made up of mountains: the Rif Mountains, Mid Atlas, High Atlas, and Anti-Atlas. The mountains actually stand as a barrier between the coastal cities and the Sahara Desert. Clouds form over the Atlantic and move west to drop rain over the oak and cedar forests of the mountains. This precipitation flows to the coastal area and trickles down into the earth to form natural aquifers. The water is used for drinking and for irrigating crops. This natural system of water delivery is very important. People wouldn't be able to live in Morocco without it.

Snowcapped Peaks

Morocco's tallest peak is located in the High Atlas. Called Jebel Toubkal, this peak rises to 13,665 feet (4,165 meters). Because of its high elevation, it is snowcapped most of the year.

When you visit a place like Morocco, you expect to find seas of sand and surf, but most people would not expect to find snow. Not many people can say they've played in the snow in Africa. So, even if you don't ski, you should at the very least go up to the mountains and slide down on a sled, stomp around in snowshoes, or toss a few snowballs at your friends. It makes for great memories and even better pictures.

There are several ski resorts in Morocco where you can ski, sled, and snowshoe. Oukaïmeden is considered the best. It is about 45 miles (72 kilometers) away from Marrakesh, which is in central Morocco. It is not as modern or fancy as resorts in Europe or North America, but it does have ski lifts, ski rentals, a small lodge, and a hotel. There is usually snow here from January to March.

Mountain Trekking

Snow sports aren't the only things to do in the Moroccan mountains, though. You can also hike, go on a mule ride, camp, visit rural villages, and see the famous Barbary macaques.

One really great place to hike is a mountainous region called the Oregano Mountains. These mountains definitely live up to their name. Wild oregano plants grow everywhere. So, as you hike, you'll smell the aroma of this sweet herb every time you brush past one. If you want to know what oregano smells like, open up your kitchen spice cabinet and give the oregano jar a whiff. It's the spice that is most commonly used on pizza.

Many people also like hiking in a place called Setti Fatma. This area is right outside of Marrakesh. There are seven sparkling waterfalls here. You'll love standing underneath these cool natural showers after hiking on a hot summer day. As you hike through this area, notice the Berber villages built on the mountainsides. You might also see women out in the streams washing the family clothes. Or, you may run across a small market where you can watch weavers hand-make colorful Berber rugs. On longer hikes, you can rent a mule to carry your sup-

FYI FACT:

Ifrane, located in the Mid Atlas Mountains in northern Morocco, is known as "Little Switzerland." It was built by the French and looks just like something you'd see in the Alps. Heavy snow falls in the winter months and it can get very cold here. In 1935, the temperature dipped to -11°F (-24°C). This is the lowest recorded temperature in all of Africa.[1]

A journey to Setti Fatma waterfalls is a daytrip from Marrakesh via 1-2 hour motorized coach ride and then a 30-minute uphill hike. The falls are fed by Atlas snow fields, so the water is cold, cold, cold!

plies, or even you. This is recommended if you plan on climbing the steep trails of such peaks as Jebel Toubkal.

If you want to see Barbary macaques in the wild, you will need to go to the Mid Atlas range. Barbary macaques are Old World monkeys. They have yellow-brown fur and pink faces, and they grow to be about 30 pounds (13 kilograms). They don't have a tail. Their arms are longer than their legs and they usually walk around on all fours. They are mainly herbivores, which means they eat plants. The Barbary macaque is a threatened species. Too many trees are being cut down in this area, which means they have fewer places to live and less food to eat.

The Moroccans tan and dye leather in the traditional way. This honeycomb with various colors reveals how they do it. Both the people and the leather get dyed here!

The Great Cities of the Plains

The great cities of the plains are Fes and Marrakesh. Fes is located in the central region of northern Morocco, and Marrakesh is located in the central region of western Morocco. They were both stopping off points on camel caravan routes long ago. When you visit here, you truly feel like you have stepped back in time to an Arab land in the middle ages.

Navigating Medieval Fes

The medina is the historic Arab section of any North African city. It is made up of winding passageways and corridors that twist together in a puzzling labyrinth. You have to know your way around a medina or you could get lost. Really lost. Medinas have restaurants, homes, schools, souks (marketplaces), mosques, *hammams* (bathhouses), and *fondouks* (inns). You can't drive a car in a medina. You can only walk or bring a donkey to haul your goods.

The medina in Fes is famous because it's the largest in the world. It is said that there are more than 9,000 streets and alleys in the Fes medina. One of the most interesting things to visit here is the tannery located in the north section of the medina.

The Chouara tannery isn't just any tannery—it's the oldest in the world. This is where the hides of animals are transformed into soft, colorful, Moroccan leather. They don't use modern technology here. Everything is done the old-fashioned way using the same methods that have been in place for centuries.

Hides are purchased from the herdsmen in the adjacent marketplace and brought into the tannery. This area looks like a giant honeycomb of circular stone tubs. Each tub contains a different type of liquid. The fur is removed, then hides are dunked into the tubs that are filled with a white milky liquid. Although the liquid looks like milk, it's actually a combination of cow urine and pigeon droppings. And if the image in your mind is enough to make you cringe, imagine how bad it must smell! But this liquid makes the hides soft and flexible.

The hides are then submerged in the dyes. All of the dyes are made from natural materials like pomegranates, saffron, poppy, indigo, and antimony. The tubs of dyes look like a giant tray of watercolors filled with reds, yellows, browns, and blues. The workers stomp the hides into the tubs with their feet until the hides soak up the bright colors. The hides aren't the only things to get dyed here. The workers' legs, feet, and arms will be stained with the colors of the dyes, too.

Once the hides are dyed, they are placed on the stone rooftop to dry. The dried leather is then used to make bags, coats, purses, and babouches.

Tourists can stand in the balconies above the tannery and watch the men work. Or, they can come down below and get a personal tour. Some choose to just stay in the balconies, though, to keep their distance from the smell.

Famous Fes Native

Rachid Yazami is a native of Fes. He is a scientist who currently lives in Singapore and works in the fields of materials science and engineering. He is a professor and scientist at the Nanyang Technological University.

Yazami is also an inventor. He has invented, or helped to invent, more than fifty different products related to the lithium battery.[1] The lithium battery is used in all sorts of products ranging from cell phones and watches to computers, digital cameras, and toys.

Yazami's research and inventions have earned him many awards from such organizations as NASA (National Aeronautics and Space Administration) and NATO (North Atlantic Treaty Organization).[2]

Magical Marrakesh

The first thing visitors notice about Marrakesh is the color of the city. The buildings are the color of orange-red paprika. That's why it's nicknamed the "Red City."

Marrakesh is an exciting place to visit. One of the most popular places to go to in Marrakesh is the souk. Souks are the marketplaces that are found in the medinas. Many Moroccan cities have a souk. But the one at Marrakesh is considered to be the best in the entire country. The narrow lanes twist and turn revealing intriguing merchandise around every corner. At one stand, rectangular orange and black Berber rugs dangle from bamboo poles. At another, a rainbow of spices are piled in pyramid shapes atop wooden barrels. Further down the corridor, painted pottery and shiny brass lamps are on display. Food vendors are everywhere. Steam billows from carts cooking juicy lamb kabobs and spicy tagine. People crowd the narrow corridors: women buying baskets of vegetables and freshly cut meat, and tourists examining silk scarves and trying on colorful babouches. Men dressed in djellabas squeeze through narrow alleyways with their donkeys loaded with goods.

If you think watching the action in the souk is fun, try buying something. Moroccans barter and haggle in the souks. And they expect everyone—locals and tourists alike—to participate. Here's how it is done. Say you want to buy a Berber rug. First, ask the shopkeeper how much it is. He'll offer you a price. You reply by offering a lower price. He'll come back with a price closer to your price. Then, you return and do the same. Finally, after working back and forth for a while, you might find a price you both agree upon. If not, you don't have to buy the rug here. Maybe another shopkeeper around the corner will offer you a better deal.

FYI FACT:

Marrakesh may be the Red City, but there's also a Blue Town, located in the Rif Mountains. It's name is Chefchaouen. The buildings in the medina are all painted different shades of blue: sky blue, cobalt blue, periwinkle blue, and turquoise blue.

A souk

Souks have just about everything that a person living in the medina could need. Locals buy what they need for their daily meals. Men stop by the food stands and buy their lunches. Souks are exciting and busy. They're a fun place to see what daily life in Marrakesh is really like.

Djemaa el Fna

The center square in Marrakesh is called Djemaa el Fna (jah-MAH-al-fuh-nah). Every evening, this place springs to life into a carnival of smells, tastes, and sights. Hundreds of food vendors set up temporary cafes. They sell lamb sausages stuffed into pitas, garlic snail soup, sheep's heads, buttery pastries, and freshly squeezed orange juice. Acrobatic troupes perform flips and stunts from high atop human pyramids. Musicians in colorful costumes play traditional Moroccan instruments. Men donning turbans sit on colorful Berber rugs and charm their snakes with the notes of their flutes. Other men strut around the square with a pet monkey wearing a felt fez hat. Women tell fortunes and paint intricate henna tattoos. Medicine men sell elixirs and pull rotten teeth with pliers. Since each booth has its own gas lantern, the festivities can last long after the sun has gone down.

Djemaa el Fna is one of the most famous things to see in Marrakesh. It simply should not be missed on a trip to the Red City.

Aït-Ben-Haddou

East of Marrakesh is an ancient walled city called Aït-Ben-Haddou (ATE-ben-hah-doo). The kasbah (fortress) in this town was originally constructed in the 11th century by Berber people. It is now a United Nations world heritage site.

A few families still live in the kasbah today. They live just the way people have done for hundreds of years. They don't have electricity or running water. The women make a pita-like bread by stretching dough over a hot stone and placing it in a small oven. The thick mud walls keep the rooms inside cool, even when it is over 100°F (38°C) outside.

Inside the kasbah is a labyrinth of dark passageways. The design of the fortress confused invaders, who could not find their way around and were easily captured. Aït-Ben-Haddou makes a great backdrop for Hollywood movies, including one you may be familiar with, *Gladiator.*

Movies, Movies, Movies

Ouarzazate (WAHR-zuh-zaht) is known for its movie studios, and visitors can take guided tours. The guides will boast that everything here is "genuine fake." They're genuine because they really were used in the movies. But they're fake because nothing is quite what it seems. For instance, you might think that a building in the studio is made of stone. But that stone is just rubber painted to look like stone. How about that wooden furniture? Nope. That's fake too. It's made out of cardboard. Surely those Egyptian Pharaoh statues are the real deal. Wrong again. They are made out of plaster and painted by artists to look like they came straight from Cairo. Don't think these tricks are unique to Morocco. This is actually exactly what you'll find in movie studios in Hollywood, too. Genuine fake.

Ouarzazate is located about 125 miles (200 kilometers) southeast of Marrakesh. It is on a high plateau south of the High Atlas Mountains. It's one of the last stopping points to buy supplies on your way to the Sahara Desert.

The rolling dunes of the Sahara are constantly changing, making for a new adventure every time you visit.

Roughing it in the Sahara

It would be a shame to travel all the way to Morocco and not visit the Sahara. That's why visitors try to spend at least one day and night, and more if they can, out on this vast desert. It's definitely a once-in-a-lifetime experience.

A journey through the Sahara begins at the base camp. This is where you'll meet your Berber guide. It's also where you'll meet your transportation, a dromedary camel. This type of camel is also known as the Arabian camel. It only has one hump, and it is a surprisingly large animal. At around 10 feet (3 meters) long, 6.5 feet (2 meters) tall, and weighing up to 1,600 pounds (725 kilograms), it's almost like a small car on stilts. They're so tall that they have to kneel down so people can climb on their backs.

Riding a camel isn't like riding any other kind of animal. For one, you know that big hump that looks like a mountain in the center of its back? That's your seat. It's a little tricky balancing on it and it's not very comfortable. Camels also sway when they walk, which is one of the reasons they call them the "ships of the desert." It almost feels like you are on a boat swaying back and forth in the water when you're on their backs. When camels walk, they actually move both legs on the same side of the body at the same time. In other words, with one step, the front and back leg on the right side will move forward. Then, with the next step, the front and back leg on the left side will move forward. This is what causes the swaying motion. The camel has big, wide feet which help him stay on top of the sand instead of sinking into it. It's kind of the same idea as a person who uses snowshoes to avoid sinking in the snow. Listen to the sounds your camel makes. Sometimes it makes gurgling noises, other times it might moan or bellow. Sometimes it even makes a low growl that sounds a little like Chewbacca from the *Star Wars* movies.

It might take you a little while to get used to riding a camel. Once you do, though, you can start to enjoy the beautiful scenery. Look out over the Sahara's velvety-soft sand and huge mountains called dunes. Some of these sand dunes can be 500 feet (150 meters) tall. The sand in some places will look white like salt, but in other places it will look brown like cinnamon or orange-red like paprika. Keep in mind that what you are seeing might never be the same way again. That's because the sand on the desert shifts constantly. Dunes rarely stay in the same place or in the same shape for very long.

After a long day of riding, you'll see an island of palms in the distance. This oasis is your campsite and it's where you will stop for the night. Once off your camel, you'll help set up your tent in camp. Then, you can go explore, but don't journey too far off. It's easy to get lost since all the scenery looks pretty much the same. One thing you'll definitely want to do is try running up one of the dunes. It's not as easy as it looks. Even if you're moving quickly, your feet will still start to sink deep into the soft sand. Now you can see why those big, wide feet on your camel are so helpful to him.

Once the golden sun sets on the western horizon, you will sit with the rest of your travelers on colorful handmade Berber rugs that might remind you of Aladdin's magic carpet. You'll share a plate of tagine and drink sweet mint tea. Your guide might tell you fascinating stories of ancient Arab tales. Or, maybe you'll get to listen to some real Moroccan music with drums and flutes. Before you head off to sleep, don't forget to look up into the sky. Without any city lights out here on the desert, the stars will be brilliant—like millions of diamonds dotting an ebony canvas. It'll be one of the most beautiful sights you'll ever see.

The next morning, wake up early so you can see the sunrise over the dunes. The sand will glisten in the early morning light. Once you've eaten your breakfast, climb aboard your desert ship. It's time to head back to base camp and civilization.

Running Across the Desert

Every April, runners from all over the world descend on Morocco. They want to be one of the few proud athletes who can say they've finished the Marathon des Sables (MDS), or Marathon of the Sands.

This race is considered one of the most difficult in the world. It's not just a regular marathon—this is an ultra-marathon. It stretches 151 miles (243 kilometers) and lasts six days. The temperatures can get as hot as 120°F (49°C), and sometimes even more.

For this race, you don't just run on paved roads or groomed trails. You trudge across gray gravel plains that resemble the surface of the moon. You struggle up and over orange sand dunes that look like the landscape of Mars. Along the way, you have to carry everything with

Racing through the Sahara is a feat only attempted by the world's top athletes. The run is grueling and exhausting and if a runner is not careful, it could also be deadly.

Mohamad Ahansal and his brother grew up racing along this treacherous terrain. Now, they compete often in this intense ultra marathon.

you: food, clothes, medical kit, water. Runners are only permitted to have a certain amount of water. The rest is provided at aid stations along the way. At night, you sleep in a goat-skin tent on a Berber rug. You eat the same freeze-dried food that astronauts eat. Your feet will blister, your body will ache, and you will probably feel sick to your stomach more than once. But every day you get up and run again. The race might be long and hard, but the only way to finish it is one step at a time.

Those who make it across the finish line say that it's the best thing they've ever done. Those who don't finish still say they're at least glad they tried.

Lahcen Ahansal has won the Marathon des Sables more times than anyone else on earth. His endurance in these extreme conditions is indeed remarkable.

Top Runners

Two of the most famous winners of the MDS are brothers Mohamad and Lahcen Ahansal. They grew up in a nomadic herding tribe in the Sahara. When they were kids, they would have to walk or run back and forth to school every day across the desert sand. Sometimes they would end up running 17 miles (28 kilometers) in one day.[1]

The brothers didn't run just to get from place to place, they also ran for fun. Their friends and family didn't understand why they would *want* to do that. They would dress in their traditional djellabas with their running clothes underneath. When they were far enough away from the village that no one could see them, they would bury their robes in the sand and then run, run, and run.[2]

All this running paid off. Lahcen is a ten-time winner of the MDS and Mohamad is a four-time winner. Lahcen is in the Guinness Book of World Records for winning the MDS more times than anyone else. He won it in 1997 and then in the years 1999-2007.[3]

FYI FACT:

Camels have two rows of eyelashes and can close their nostrils completely. This helps them keep out sand during a sandstorm. They can sometimes have bad breath because of how their stomach digests the food they eat. Camels are also known to spit at their enemies.

Djemaa el Fna is a delight for the senses and a must see for visitors to Marrakesh.

Dreaming
of Morocco

When people visit a new country, they should take some time to learn about the country's customs. Learning these things will help people avoid embarrassing themselves and offending others.

Here's what you need to know about Morocco's customs:

- Moroccans shake hands when they meet new people. They only kiss family and close friends on the cheek.
- Moroccans dress conservatively and modestly. Visitors should do the same by wearing shirts with sleeves and long pants or skirts.
- Moroccans remove their shoes when they enter someone's house.
- Moroccans wash their hands with a pitcher of water at the table before they eat their food.
- Moroccans never eat with their left hand, only their right. The left hand is used for bathroom duties only.
- Moroccans eat out of a shared bowl or dish, but they only eat out of the part of the dish that is closest to them.

Morocco is a beautiful country with friendly people, fascinating places to visit, delicious food, and a fun and interesting culture. Many people dream of the day that they can visit this beautiful country. Now that you've read this book, maybe you'll want to visit Morocco, too!

Moroccan Couscous

Serves: 8 people

Ingredients:

1¼ teaspoons ground cumin
½ teaspoon ground ginger
¼ teaspoon ground cloves
⅛ teaspoon ground cayenne pepper
½ teaspoon ground cardamom
¼ teaspoon ground coriander
¼ teaspoon ground allspice
1 tablespoon olive oil
1 red onion, diced
1 red, green, or yellow bell pepper, diced
2 zucchinis, diced
½ cup golden raisins
1 teaspoon salt
  grated zest of one orange
1 (14.5-ounce) can garbanzo beans, rinsed and drained
1½ cups chicken broth
½ cup orange juice
1½ cups couscous
3 tablespoons fresh mint, chopped

Directions:

1. **With adult supervision**, place a large pot over medium heat.
2. Add the spices (cumin, ginger, cloves, cayenne pepper, cardamom, coriander, and allspice) to the pot and toast for 2-3 minutes until fragrant.
3. Stir in oil and onion. Cook until softened, about 5 minutes.
4. Stir in bell pepper, zucchini. Cook for 5 minutes.
5. Stir in raisins, salt, orange zest, garbanzo beans, chicken broth, and orange juice.
6. Turn heat to high. Bring to a boil.
7. Remove from heat. Stir in couscous.
8. Cover. Let stand for 5 minutes.
9. Fluff with a fork. Then, stir in the chopped mint.

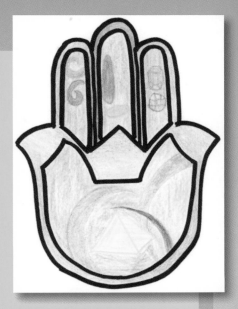

Hamsa Bookmark

Many people believe in symbols for good luck. There are four-leaf clovers, rainbows, horseshoes, and rabbits' feet. Moroccans believe that an open hand, called a hamsa, is a lucky symbol. The hamsa isn't just any hand. It's supposed to represent the hand of Fatima. She was the daughter of the Prophet Muhammad and an important person in Islamic history. This hand is said to serve as a protection to all those who own it and will also give them good luck.

Hamsas are decorated in many ways. Some are decorated with black, swirly designs. Some are decorated in bright colors. Some have flowers, hearts, fish, and animals on them. Some just have geometric designs.

Here's how to make your own hamsa that you can use as a good-luck bookmark.

Materials
the outline of this hamsa found on this page
plain white piece of paper
crayons, markers, glitter, sequins, or anything you want to use to decorate your hamsa

Directions
1. Trace the outline of this pattern onto a piece of plain white paper.
2. Then, decorate it anyway you choose. You can use crayons, markers, paint, glitter, sequins, etc. Use your imagination and make one that is unique and incorporates your personality.
3. When you are all done, use it as a bookmark, wall hanging, or in any place you'd like to bring good luck.

B.C.E.

before 800	Berbers inhabit North Africa. Many live in what is now Morocco.
ca. 800	Phoenicians settle in Morocco and set up trade routes.
500	Carthaginians take over Morocco, expanding the trade routes started by the Phoenicians.
146	Carthage falls to Rome.

C.E.

40	The area of modern-day Morocco becomes a Roman province known as Mauritania Tingitana. Volubilis becomes the Roman capital of the province.
278	Romans move their capital to Tangier.
429	Vandals take over Mauritania Tingitana, ending Roman rule there.
533	Byzantines defeat the Vandals for control of Mauritania Tingitana, rebuilding the Roman ruins there.
682	Arabs invade North Africa. Islam eventually becomes the main religion there.
788-923	Morocco is controlled by Arab rulers, the Idrisid Dynasty. Idris II designates Fes as the capital.
ca. 1046	Hilalians from the Arabian peninsula move into North Africa. Arabs become part of the population in Morocco.
1062	Morocco is ruled by the Berber Almoravid Dynasty, whose capital is Marrakesh.
1147	The Almohads (Berbers) defeat the Almoravid king, taking over as the ruling dynasty in Morocco.
1244	Nomadic Berbers called the Merenid take over Fes, making it their capital. They continue battling for control further into Morocco.
1465	The Wattasid Dynasty takes over Morocco.
1509	The Saadian Dynasty rules southern Morocco.
1554	The Saadians defeat the Wattasids at the Battle of Tadla, extending their control further north.
1669	The Alaouite Dynasty takes control of Morocco. This family still rules Morocco today.

1894	Hassan I, the last effective sultan of "Old Morocco," dies.
1912	The Treaty of Fes gives control of Morocco to France and Spain, dividing it into two protectorates.
1921	Moroccan natives form The Republic of the Rif and declare independence from Spain.
1926	The Republic of the Rif is defeated by French and Spanish forces.
1939-1945	Morocco assists the Allies in World War II. During the war, Moroccans demand their independence from France. French leadership refuses to give up control.
1956	Morocco gains independence from France and Spain. Sultan Mohammed V is king.
1961	King Mohammed dies. His son, Hassan II, becomes king.
1963	The first democratic elections are held in Morocco.
1975	By orders of the king, thousands of Moroccans march into what is now called Western Sahara to claim it as part of Morocco. The borders of this territory are still being disputed.
1976	Morocco and Algeria battle over Western Sahara.
1992	Morocco's constitution is changed. More power is given to the Prime Minister and Parliament.
1999	King Hassan II dies. His son, Mohammed VI, becomes king.
2003	Suicide bombers attack Jewish and Spanish sites in Casablanca.
2004	A powerful earthquake hits Morocco, killing more than 500 people. This same year a free trade agreement is signed with the United States.
2007	Suicide bombers strike again in Casablanca.
2011	People begin protesting in the cities. They want to limit the king's power and improve the constitution in favor of the people. Another bomb attack, this time at a cafe in Marrakesh. Moroccans vote in favor of a the new constitution proposed by King Mohammed VI.
2012	Morocco's football team wins the Arab Nations Cup.

Chapter 1. The Hollywood of North Africa

1. Tom Nugent, *Sarah Lawrence Magazine,* "Sanaa Hamri '96 Direction," Spring 2006. http://www.slc.edu/magazine/coeducation/mag_coed-glimpse_hamri.php

2. Nicole Marie Richardson, *Black Enterprise,* "Sanaa Hamri," vol. 37, issue 5, December 2006.

Chapter 2. A Rich History and Government

1. Oren Dorell, *USA Today,* "Morocco's Constitution Could Hold Lessons in Arab World," July 4, 2011. http://www.usatoday.com/news/world/2011-07-04-morocco-vote-reforms_n.htm

Chapter 4. At Home in Morocco

1. Richard Hamilton, BBC, "The Story-tellers of Marrakesh," February 19, 2007. http://news.bbc.co.uk/2/hi/programmes/from_our_own_correspondent/6368057.stm

Chapter 5. From Sea to Shining Sea

1. Craig Whitlock, *The Washington Post,* "A 'Chunnel' for Spain and Morocco," January 28, 2007. http://www.washingtonpost.com/wp-dyn/content/article/2007/01/27/AR2007012701334.html

Chapter 6. Mountain Peaks and Berber Villages

1. Arizona State University, *World Weather/Climate Extremes Archive,* "Africa: Lowest Temperature," http://wmo.asu.edu/africa-lowest-temperature

Chapter 7. The Great Cities of the Plains

1. Nanyang Technological University, "Visiting Staff: Professor Rachid Yazami," http://www.mse.ntu.edu.sg/AboutUs/Organisation/Pages/VisitingStaff.aspx#rachid

2. Ibid.

Chapter 8. Roughing it in the Sahara

1. Christian Madsen, Ultrarun.com, "The Sandman," http://ultrarun.com/en/2010/06/manden-fra-%C3%B8rkenen/#.UCVQ2BGjSig.google

2. Jacqueline Kantor, *The New York Times,* "On the Run in the Sahara, for 153 Miles," April 6, 2012. http://www.nytimes.com/2012/04/07/sports/runnings-ultimate-test-153-miles-in-the-sahara.html?_r=1&pagewanted=all

3. Guinness World Records: "Most Marathon de Sables Wins," http://www.guinnessworldrecords.com/world-records/12000/most-marathon-des-sables-wins

Books
Cassanos, Lynda Cohen. *Major Muslim Nations: Morocco*. Broomall, PA: Mason Crest Publishers, 2010.
Hunter, Nick. *Countries Around the World: Morocco*. Chicago, IL: Heinemann Library, 2012.
Nelson, Robin. *Morocco*. Minneapolis, MN: Lerner Publishing Group, 2012.
Wolfert, Paula. *The Food of Morocco*. New York: Ecco, 2011.

On the Internet:
Country Reports: "Morocco," http://www.countryreports.org/country/Morocco.htm
Morocco.com: Morocco Channel, http://www.morocco.com
National Geographic: Morocco Guide, http://travel.nationalgeographic.com/travel/countries/
     morocco-guide/
Time For Kids, Around the World: "Morocco," http://www.timeforkids.com/destination/morocco

WORKS CONSULTED

Arizona State University: *World Weather/Climate Extremes Archive,* "Africa: Lowest Temperature,"
     http://wmo.asu.edu/africa-lowest-temperature
Central Intelligence Agency: *The World Factbook,* "Morocco,"
     https://www.cia.gov/library/publications/the-world-factbook/geos/mo.html
Dorell, Oren. "Morocco's Constitution Could Hold Lessons in Arab World." *USA Today,* July 4, 2011.
     http://www.usatoday.com/news/world/2011-07-04-morocco-vote-reforms_n.htm
Fabricant, Florence. "The Fragrant Food of Morocco." *The New York Times,* December 6, 1992.
     http://www.nytimes.com/1992/12/06/travel/the-fragrant-food-of-morocco.
     html?pagewanted=all&src=pm
Fodor's Travel Intelligence: "Morocco Travel Guide," http://www.fodors.com/world/africa-and-middle-
     east/morocco/
Frommer's: "Morocco," http://www.frommers.com/destinations/morocco/
Frommer's: *Morocco,* "Arts & Crafts," http://www.frommers.com/destinations/morocco/3871020557.
     html
Guinness World Records: "Most Marathon de Sables Wins," http://www.guinnessworldrecords.com/
     world-records/12000/most-marathon-des-sables-wins
Hamilton, Richard. "The Story-tellers of Marrakesh." BBC, February 19, 2007. http://news.bbc.co.
     uk/2/hi/programmes/from_our_own_correspondent/6368057.stm
Kantor, Jacqueline. "On the Run in the Sahara, for 153 Miles." *The New York Times,* April 6, 2012.
     http://www.nytimes.com/2012/04/07/sports/runnings-ultimate-test-153-miles-in-the-sahara.
     html?_r=1&pagewanted=all
Lonely Planet: *Thorn Tree Travel Forum,* "Morocco," http://www.lonelyplanet.com/thorntree/forum.
     jspa?forumID=9&keywordid=35
Madsen, Christian. "The Sandman." Ultrarun.com, http://ultrarun.com/en/2010/06/manden-fra-
     %C3%B8rkenen/#.UCVQ2BGjSig.google
Nanyang Technological University: "Visiting Staff: Professor Rachid Yazami," http://www.mse.ntu.
     edu.sg/AboutUs/Organisation/Pages/VisitingStaff.aspx#rachid
National Geographic: "Morocco Guide," http://travel.nationalgeographic.com/travel/countries/
     morocco-guide/
Nugent, Tom. "Sanaa Hamri '96 Direction." *Sarah Lawrence Magazine,* Spring 2006. http://www.slc.
     edu/magazine/coeducation/mag_coed-glimpse_hamri.php
Richardson, Nicole Marie. "Sanaa Hamri." *Black Enterprise,* December 2006.
Ross, John F. "Monkey in the Middle." *Smithsonian,* March 2004. http://www.smithsonianmag.com/
     science-nature/monkey.html
Sacred Destinations: "Morocco Glossary," http://www.sacred-destinations.com/morocco/morocco-
     glossary.htm
Vlahides, John. "Skiing in Morocco." *Lonely Planet,* October 22, 2009. http://www.lonelyplanet.com/
     africa/travel-tips-and-articles/11909
Whitlock, Craig. "A 'Chunnel' for Spain and Morocco." *The Washington Post,* January 28, 2007. http://
     www.washingtonpost.com/wp-dyn/content/article/2007/01/27/AR2007012701334.html
Wilder, Charly. "36 Hours in Marrakesh, Morocco." *The New York Times,* December 23, 2010. http://
     travel.nytimes.com/2010/12/26/travel/26marrakesh-hours.html

babouche (buh-BOOSH): a type of colorful leather shoe that originated in Morocco.

couscous (KOOS-koos): a Berber dish of semolina (hard wheat) that is traditionally served with a meat or vegetable stew spooned over it (like tagine). It is a staple food of North Africa.

djellaba (juh-LAH-buh): an ankle-length loose robe with long sleeves and a hood that is traditionally worn in Muslim countries by both men and women. These are usually made out of yarn or fine wool for men and cotton or silk for women.

fez (fehz): a man's felt hat in the shape of a flat-topped cone common in North Africa. It's usually red with a black tassel hanging from the top.

fondouk (fohn-DOOK): traditional travelers' inn that also serves as a storehouse for goods.

hammam (huh-MAHM): public bathhouse common in Islamic countries.

jebel (JEB-ull): mountain.

kasbah (KAZ-buh): ancient walled fortress made of mud bricks that includes a city, medina, and the home of the tribal leader which would be similar in purpose to a European castle. They were often built on a hill and surrounded by high walls.

medina (meh-DEE-nuh): the old Arab or non-European part of a North African town designed in a labyrinth of narrow alleyways and corridors only wide enough for foot or donkey traffic. Traditionally, this is where the houses, souks, and craftsmen's workshops were found clustered around public buildings such as the mosque, fondouk, communal fountain, and hammam.

minaret (min-uh-RET): the tall tower on a mosque used to call people to prayer.

mosque (mahsk): Muslim place of worship.

riad (REE-ahd): house built around a courtyard; today many are used as hotels and restaurants.

souk or souq (sook): marketplace.

tagine or tajine (tah-JEEN): traditional Moroccan dish that is named after the clay pot in which it is cooked. It is a stew-like dish that is usually made with chicken or lamb and a combination of such ingredients as olives, quinces, apples, pears, apricots, raisins, prunes, dates, nuts, fresh or preserved lemons, honey, ground cinnamon, saffron, ginger, turmeric, cumin, paprika, and pepper.

agriculture   13, 21-22, 37, 39
Ahansal, Lahcen   53
Ahansal, Mohamad   52, 53
Aït-Ben-Haddou   47
Alaouite Dynasty   18
Al-Karaouine Mosque and University   24, 25
American Legation   34
Arabic   9, 13, 21
architecture   28, 37, 40, 45, 47
Atlantic Ocean   12, 17, 21, 33, 36, 37, 39
Atlas Lions   13, 30-31
Atlas Mountains   33, 38, 39, 40, 41, 47
Bennani, Salma   23
Berbers   13, 15-17, 21, 31, 40, 47, 49
camel   6, 12, 15, 26-27, 43, 49-51, 53
Casablanca   13, 20, 21, 29, 35-37
Casablanca (movie)   35-36
Ceuta   34
Chefchaouen   45
Christianity   13
climate   10, 12, 13, 15, 39, 40, 51
clothing   16, 22-23, 45, 55
cuisine   27-28, 37, 45, 46, 50
culture   12, 25, 27-28, 31, 55
Djemaa el Fna   46, 54
Draa River   13
economy   13, 17, 21-22, 35-36
education   18, 23, 24, 25
Essaouira   37
Fes   23, 24, 43-44
films   9-10, 47
football (soccer)   13, 30-31
France   17-18, 20, 28, 33, 34, 40
French (language)   13, 21
Garden of the Hesperides   17, 19
geography   6, 10, 12, 33, 38-41, 48, 50
government   9, 13, 18-19
Greece   17, 19
Hamri, Sanaa   9-10
Hassan II   18-19
Hassan II Mosque   29, 36
Hesperides   19
holidays   28-29
ibn Nafi, Uqba   17
Ifrane   13, 40
independence   18
Islam   10, 13, 17, 18, 21, 22, 24, 25, 28-30, 36

Israel   19
Jebel Toubkal   13, 38, 39, 41
Judaism   13, 19
kasbah   34, 47
languages   9, 13, 21
Larache (Lixus)   17
Marathon des Sables   51-53
Marrakesh   6-7, 30, 39, 40, 41, 43, 45-46, 47, 54
medina   26, 43, 45-46
Mediterranean Sea   8, 17, 21, 33, 34
Mohammed VI   19, 23, 35
Moussems   30
Muhammad   10, 18, 30
music   10, 29, 30, 31, 46, 50
nomads   14, 15, 53
oasis   15, 50
Oregano Mountains   40
Ouarzazate   13, 47
Phoenicians   17
phosphates   13, 22
Rabat   13, 18, 23, 35
Ramadan   28-29
religion   10, 13, 17, 18, 21, 22, 24, 25, 28-30, 36
Rif Mountains   16, 33, 39, 45
Rome   17, 23
Sahara Desert   6, 10, 12, 15, 27, 33, 39, 47-53
Setti Fatma   40, 41
skiing   12, 39-40
souks   31, 43, 45-46
Spain   7, 8, 17, 21, 28, 33-34
storytellers (halakis)   31
Straits of Gibraltar   26, 33-34
surfing   12, 37
Tangier   8, 9, 17, 34, 35
tannery   42, 43-44
television   10
tourism   12, 21, 33-51
transportation   25, 26-27, 32, 33, 43, 49
United States   9-10, 27, 34, 35, 37
Vandals   17
Visigoths   17
Volubilis   23
Western Sahara   22
wildlife   6, 13, 30, 41
Yazami, Rachid   44

Amie Jane Leavitt is an accomplished author and photographer. In addition, she's an adventurer who loves to travel the globe in search of interesting story ideas and beautiful places to capture on film. She has authored more than fifty books for children and has been widely published in online media and magazines. Amie particularly enjoyed researching and writing this book on Morocco. She loves the Moroccan culture and people and hopes this book will help children gain a better understanding of this beautiful African nation. To see a complete listing of Amie's current projects and published works, visit her website at www.amiejaneleavitt.com.